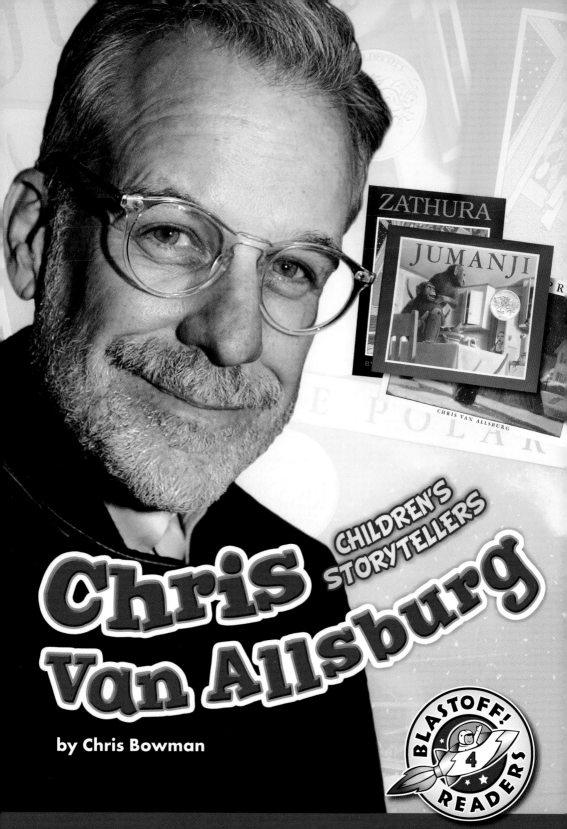

CHILDREN'S STORYTELLERS

# Chris Van Allsburg

by Chris Bowman

BLASTOFF! READERS
4

BELLWETHER MEDIA · MINNEAPOLIS, MN

Note to Librarians, Teachers, and Parents:

**Blastoff! Readers** are carefully developed by literacy experts and combine standards-based content with developmentally appropriate text.

**Level 1** provides the most support through repetition of high-frequency words, light text, predictable sentence patterns, and strong visual support.

**Level 2** offers early readers a bit more challenge through varied simple sentences, increased text load, and less repetition of high-frequency words.

**Level 3** advances early-fluent readers toward fluency through increased text and concept load, less reliance on visuals, longer sentences, and more literary language.

**Level 4** builds reading stamina by providing more text per page, increased use of punctuation, greater variation in sentence patterns, and increasingly challenging vocabulary.

**Level 5** encourages children to move from "learning to read" to "reading to learn" by providing even more text, varied writing styles, and less familiar topics.

Whichever book is right for your reader, Blastoff! Readers are the perfect books to build confidence and encourage a love of reading that will last a lifetime!

This edition first published in 2017 by Bellwether Media, Inc.

No part of this publication may be reproduced in whole or in part without written permission of the publisher. For information regarding permission, write to Bellwether Media, Inc., Attention: Permissions Department, 5357 Penn Avenue South, Minneapolis, MN 55419.

Library of Congress Cataloging-in-Publication Data

Names: Bowman, Chris, 1990- author.
Title: Chris Van Allsburg / by Chris Bowman.
Description: Minneapolis, MN : Bellwether Media, Inc., [2017] | Series: Blastoff! Readers: Children's Storytellers | Includes bibliographical references and index.
Identifiers: LCCN 2016032036 (print) | LCCN 2016042451 (ebook) | ISBN 9781626175495 (hardcover : alk. paper) | ISBN 9781681032962 (ebook)
Subjects: LCSH: Van Allsburg, Chris–Juvenile literature. | Authors, American–20th century–Biography–Juvenile literature. | Illustrators–United States–Biography–Juvenile literature. | Children's stories–Authorship–Juvenile literature. | Children's stories–Illustrations–Juvenile literature.
Classification: LCC PS3572.A41367 Z56 2017 (print) | LCC PS3572.A41367 (ebook) | DDC 813/.54 [B] –dc23
LC record available at https://lccn.loc.gov/2016032036

# Table of Contents

# Who Is Chris Van Allsburg?

Chris Van Allsburg is an award-winning children's author and **illustrator**. He has written almost 20 books in his nearly 40-year **career**.

Chris's books are known for their creative stories and beautiful artwork. His two most famous books, *Jumanji* and *The Polar Express*, have won **Caldecott Medals**.

"I always try to create something strange or puzzling in each picture."
Chris Van Allsburg

Chris was born on June 18, 1949, in Grand Rapids, Michigan. He grew up with his parents and older sister, Karen.

Grand Rapids, Michigan

"When I tell myself a story, I see it in my imagination, like a short movie."
Chris Van Allsburg

When he was young, Chris liked to draw.
He also built model airplanes, boats, and
cars. In school, Chris was mostly interested
in math and science classes.

Chris did not take art in high school. But he decided to study it in college. At first, he had a tough time in his new classes.

Then he began to study **sculpture**. This art form combined Chris's love of building models with his creative mind. It was a perfect fit!

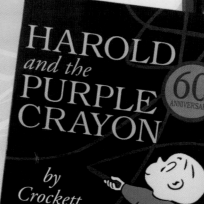

## fun fact

One of Chris's favorite books growing up was *Harold and the Purple Crayon* by Crockett Johnson.

"As long as I can remember, I've always loved to draw."
Chris Van Allsburg

After college, Chris continued to study sculpture. He moved to Rhode Island for **graduate school**. There, he set up a studio for his art.

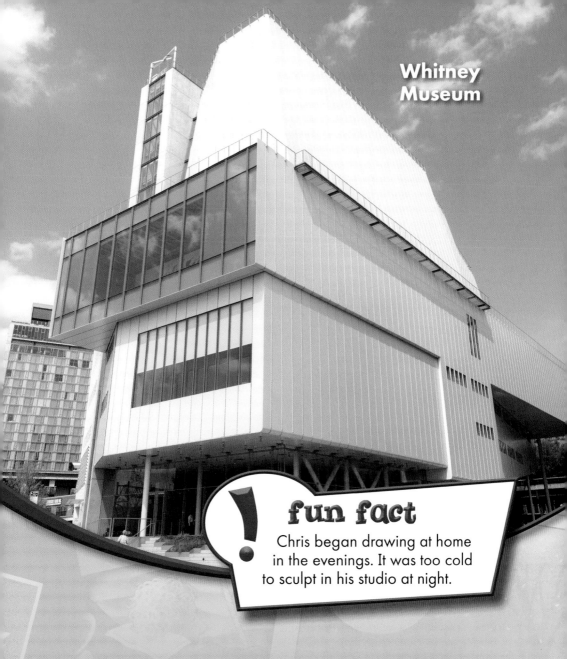

Whitney Museum

**fun fact**

Chris began drawing at home in the evenings. It was too cold to sculpt in his studio at night.

Chris also began drawing seriously. Some of his drawings were shown at the famous Whitney Museum in New York City. This gave Chris confidence to draw more.

Meanwhile, Chris married an elementary school art teacher named Lisa. She used picture books to teach her students. She thought Chris would be a good illustrator.

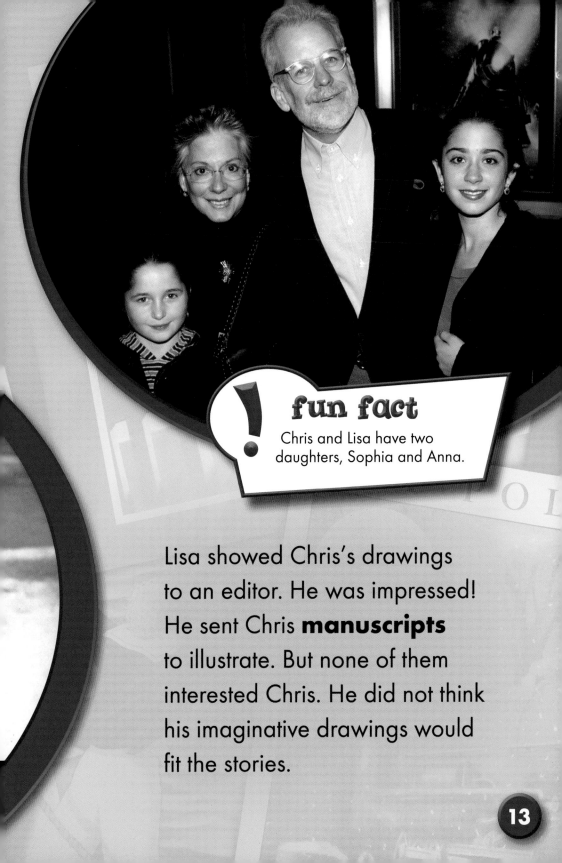

Lisa showed Chris's drawings to an editor. He was impressed! He sent Chris **manuscripts** to illustrate. But none of them interested Chris. He did not think his imaginative drawings would fit the stories.

THE GARDEN OF ABDUL GASAZI

Written and Illustrated by CHRIS VAN ALLSBURG

Chris still made sculptures, but he decided to try writing his own story to illustrate. The story he invented became his first book, *The Garden of Abdul Gasazi.*

Readers loved it! The book received a Caldecott Honor Medal. Since then, Chris has written many more picture books. He has also illustrated three books for another author.

**fun fact**

It takes Chris between seven and nine months to write a story and draw the pictures for his books.

15

# Imagine That

Most of Chris's books are **fantasies**. The stories often begin in normal places. But then Chris asks himself a question. What if strange things happen in regular life? This leads Chris's characters on **extraordinary** adventures.

## ! fun fact

Chris includes a white dog in all of his books. It is a bull terrier named Fritz.

# SELECTED WORKS

*The Garden of Abdul Gasazi* (1979)

*Jumanji* (1981)

*The Wreck of the Zephyr* (1983)

*The Mysteries of Harris Burdick* (1984)

*The Polar Express* (1985)

*The Wretched Stone* (1991)

*The Sweetest Fig* (1993)

*Zathura* (2002)

*Probuditi!* (2006)

*Queen of the Falls* (2011)

*The Misadventures of Sweetie Pie* (2014)

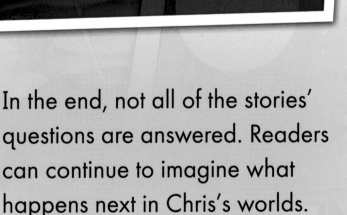

In the end, not all of the stories' questions are answered. Readers can continue to imagine what happens next in Chris's worlds.

ron
actor
one
ge
st,
ndow.
robe.
out

luctor
m.
you

Pole of
. "This
took
and he

His books are known for their **realistic** artwork. Chris wants to make impossible events look normal. He combines average places with unexpected events. In his stories, a train stops on a neighborhood street, or wild animals run around a house.

Chris does this to blur real life with imagination. He wants kids to think creatively.

## POP CULTURE CONNECTION

A film version of *Jumanji* came out in 1995. In 2017, the story will come to theaters again. Dwayne Johnson, Jack Black, and Kevin Hart are starring in a new version.

"When a story is about strange and incredible events, I think it's important that the pictures convince the reader that the events described actually could happen."
Chris Van Allsburg

Chris's stories have become **classics** for young readers. Millions of readers have gone on adventures with his characters. They travel to the North Pole in *The Polar Express* or into space with *Zathura*.

"Ideas for stories are all around."
Chris Van Allsburg

# IMPORTANT DATES

**1949:** Chris is born on June 18.

**1979:** Chris's first book, *The Garden of Abdul Gasazi*, is published.

**1980:** *The Garden of Abdul Gasazi* receives the Caldecott Honor Medal.

**1982:** The Caldecott Medal is given to *Jumanji*.

**1982:** The National Book Award for Book Illustration is given to *Jumanji*.

**1983:** *The Wreck of the Zephyr* makes the *New York Times* lists for Best Illustrated Children's Books and Outstanding Books.

**1984:** The *New York Times* includes *The Mysteries of Harris Burdick* on its Best Illustrated Children's Books list.

**1986:** *The Polar Express* wins the Caldecott Medal.

**1993:** The Regina Medal for lifetime achievement in children's literature is awarded to Chris.

**2009:** Chris receives the Society of Illustrators Original Art Lifetime Achievement Award.

The Wreck of the *Zephyr* Written and Illustrated by CHRIS VAN ALLSBURG

His stories continue to teach kids the importance of imagination!

# Glossary

**Caldecott Medals**—awards given each year to the best-illustrated children's book in America; the Caldecott Medal is given to first place and Caldecott Honors are given to the runners-up.

**career**—a job someone does for a long time

**classics**—works that will remain popular for a long time because of their excellence

**extraordinary**—going beyond what is usual

**fantasies**—stories that take place in an imaginative world

**graduate school**—a place to continue studying after college

**illustrator**—an artist who draws pictures for books

**manuscripts**—the original copies of written works before they are printed

**realistic**—like real life

**sculpture**—an art form created by molding, carving, or casting substances

# To Learn More

## AT THE LIBRARY

Bowman, Chris. *Maurice Sendak*. Minneapolis, Minn.: Bellwether Media, 2016.

Van Allsburg, Chris. *Jumanji*. Boston, Mass.: Houghton Mifflin, 2011.

Wheeler, Jill C. *Chris Van Allsburg*. Edina, Minn.: ABDO Pub. Co., 2005.

## ON THE WEB

Learning more about Chris Van Allsburg is as easy as 1, 2, 3.

1. Go to www.factsurfer.com.

2. Enter "Chris Van Allsburg" into the search box.

3. Click the "Surf" button and you will see a list of related web sites.

With factsurfer.com, finding more information is just a click away.

# Index

The images in this book are reproduced through the courtesy of: Steve Porter, front cover (books), pp. 4 (books), 8, 14, 16-17 (interiors/books), 21. ZUMA Press, Inc./ Alamy Stock Photo, front cover, p. 10; Andrea Renault/ Globe Photos/ZUMAPRESS.com, pp. 4-5; Associated Press/ AP Images, pp. 6-7, 15; Richard Howard/ The LIFE Images Collection/ Getty Images, pp. 8-9, 12-13, 14-15, 20; Osugi, pp. 10-11; SETH WENIG/ REUTERS/ Newscom, p. 13; Carol VanHook/ Flickr, pp. 18-19.